Women Boxers **The New Warriors**

Publication of *Women Boxers: The New Warriors* is funded in part by grants from the City of Houston through the Cultural Arts Council of Houston/Harris County, the Clayton Fund and by the Exemplar Program, a program of Americans for the Arts in collaboration with the LarsonAllen Public Services Group, funded by the Ford Foundation. We are grateful for their support.

Recovering the past, creating the future

Arte Público Press
University of Houston
452 Cullen Performance Hall
Houston, Texas 77204-2004

Book design Small Project Office

Montoya, Delilah.
    Women Boxers: The New Warriors / photographs by Delilah Montoya; with essays by María Teresa Márquez and C. Odine Chavoya.
        p. cm.
    ISBN-10: 1-55885-475-4 (alk. paper)
    ISBN-13: 978-1-55885-475-8
    1. Women boxers—United States—Portraits. 2. Women boxers—United States. I. Márquez, María Teresa. II. Chavoya, C. Odine. III. Title.
GV1136.3.M66 2006
796.83082—dc22   2005057115

∞ The paper used in this publication meets the requirements of the American National Standard for Permanence of Paper for Printed Library Materials Z39.48-1984.

Copyright © 2006 by Delilah Montoya
Printed in the United States of America

6 7 8 9 0 1 2 3 4 5   0 9 8 7 6 5 4 3 2 1

Women Boxers **The New Warriors**

Photographs by

Delilah Montoya

with Essays by

María Teresa Márquez
and
C. Ondine Chavoya

Dedication

To the memory of Rodolfo "Corky" Gonzales, June 18, 1928–April 12, 2005,
a National Amateur Athletic Union Bantamweight Champion and revolutionary Chicano activist who hung up his gloves
to lead his people down the path of justice.

Essays

No Longer Counted Out: Fighting Isn't What It Used to Be
María Teresa Márquez
9

Women Boxers: The New Warriors
Delilah Montoya
19

Malcriada Delilah Montoya Photographer
C. Ondine Chavoya
90

Las Malcriadas' Profiles

Super Flyweight
1 **Mónica Lovato**
24

Super Flyweight
2 **Jodie Esquibel**
28

Bantamweight
3 **María Lucy Contreras**
32

Super Bantamweight
4 **Jackie Chávez**
36

Super Bantamweight
5 **Terri "Lil' Loca" Lynn Cruz**
42

Super Featherweight
6 **Elisha Olivas**
48

Lightweight
7 **Mia "The Knockout" St. John**
54

Light Welterweight
8 **Stephanie "Golden Girl" Jaramillo**
60

Light Welterweight
9 **Holly Holm**
66

Welterweight
10 **Christy "Coalminer's Daughter" Martin**
78

Light Middleweight
11 **Akondaye "Storm" Fountain**
82

Super Middleweight
12 **Yolanda "Stone Hands" Swindell**
86

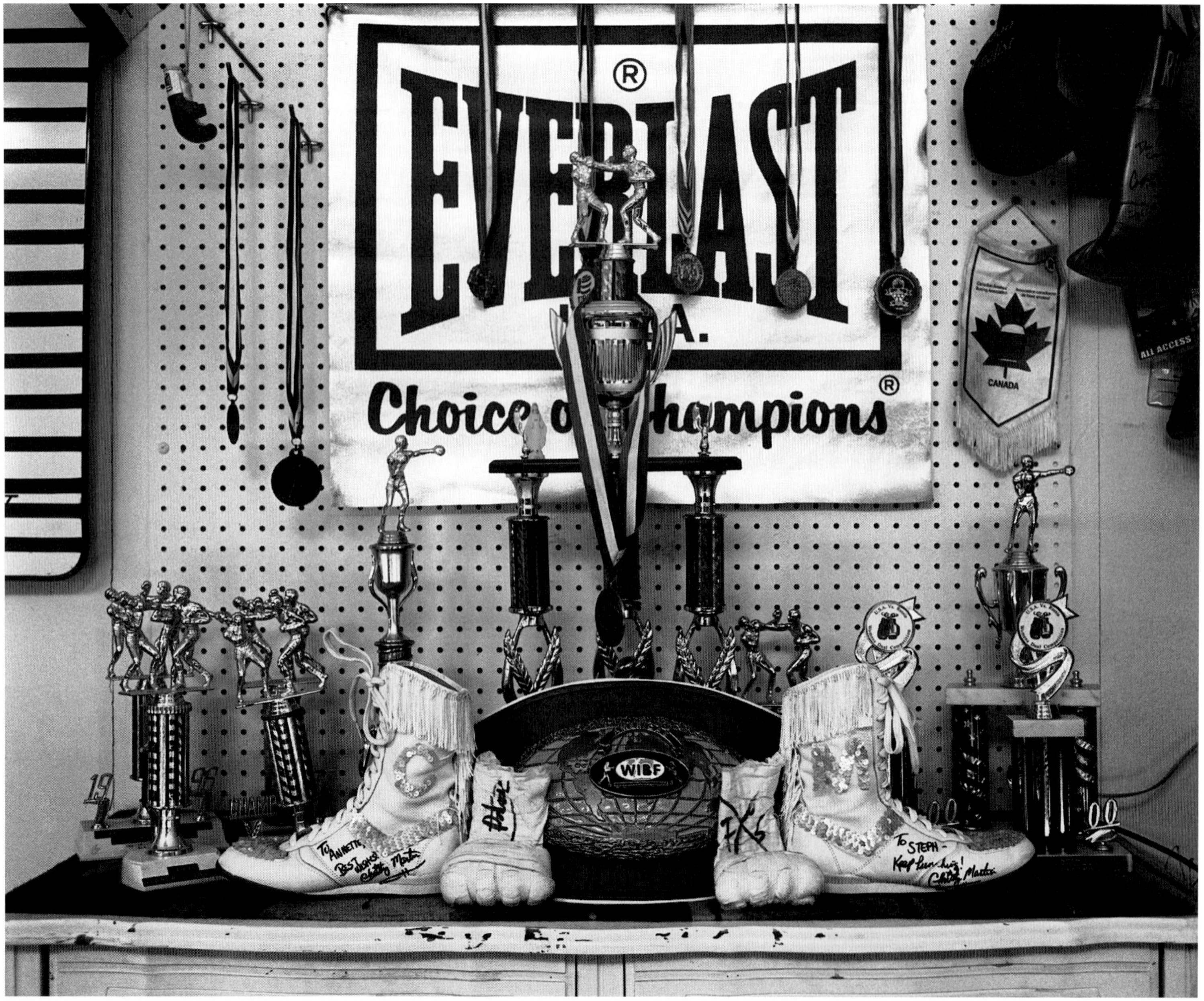
EVERLAST
Choice
hampions
CANADA
ALL ACCESS
WIBF
To STEPH -

Acknowledgements

First of all, our thanks go to those *malcriadas*, hard-working women boxers taking chances to expand the tradition of professional and amateur boxing. We would like to thank all the members of the boxing community who helped us obtain the material necessary for this book. Special thanks go to Chris Cozzone, a sports journalist and staff member of www.insidewomensboxing.com, who generously shared useful advice and reliable data. We are obliged to John Sheppard at www.boxrec.com for maintaining a website that provided the statistics on the boxers represented in this book. Promoters such as Fire Inside Productions, Ross Sánchez in coordination with Ohkay Casino; Fresquez Productions Inc., Lenny Fresquez in coordination with Isleta Casino; Sky Ute Promotions; Ben Fernández at the Sky Ute Casino; Sugar Ray Leonard Boxing, Sugar Ray Leonard in coordination with Sandia Casino and the Reliant Center Promotions kindly issued credentials so that Teresa Márquez and I could record the fights. Many thanks to trainers Ray Ontiveros, Mike Winkeljohn, Steve Maestas and Sergio Chávez, who opened their gyms and offered their views to help us understand their boxers' efforts. This book was produced in part by funding provided by the Cultural Arts Council of Houston and Harris County Individual Artist Grant Program and the University of Houston Small Grants Program. We are grateful for their contributions.

2005 Albuquerque, New Mexico
Stephanie Jaramillo's Trophy Shrine

No Longer Counted Out
Fighting Isn't What It Used to Be

María Teresa Márquez, University of New Mexico

The female boxer is monstrous! That is the claim of Joyce Carol Oates, author of the classic 1987 collection of essays about the "sweet science," *On Boxing*. Yes, women boxers *are* monstrous. They have been forced to become monsters by a society that justifies the subjugation of women within various systems of power. Female boxers are courageous; by stepping into the ring they challenge the social, cultural, and political barriers established to maintain male dominance in society.

Women boxers do not just fight one another; they fight against the belief that it is unnatural for a woman to be athletic, strong, aggressive, and confident in a sport historically dominated by males. Yet, many female boxers are mothers. Some are single parents with extended families to support. They are nurturing, loving, and want the best for their families, friends, and aspiring female boxers.

Yes, women boxers *are* monstrous. The female boxer is serious, brave, strong, and bold. She is committed to the arduous training demanded of the serious fighter; she flexes her physical prowess in one of the most brutal and violent sports.

Boxing, in its genesis, attracted women willing to fight bare-fisted to the bloody end, with biting, scratching, and hair pulling. In London, *The Daily Post* of October 7, 1728, reported a verbal exchange between Elizabeth Stokes, the self-acclaimed European champion, and Ann Field, an ass driver. Stokes and Fields announced they were willing to enter the boxing ring to trounce and pummel each other for ten pounds. Eighteenth-century female fighters drew frenzied, rowdy crowds eager to gawk at female pugilists as they battered each other in brutal brawls. Perhaps the sight of women uncorseted to the waist, and draped in light shifts that might be torn to shreds in the combat, aroused the fans.

2005 Okay Casino, Espanola, New Mexico
Audrey Vela's Corner

Women boxers, also scantily clad, flaunted the Victorian dress code in the first reported American bout, in 1888, in Buffalo, New York. Unfortunately, women in such dishabille were not seen as representing serious female athleticism, especially when the bouts were in saloons, brothels, and on the vaudeville circuit. Undoubtedly, the women who entered the ring to entertain were of ill-repute, claims Allen Guttmann in his 1991 study, *Women's Sports: A History*.

From America's beginnings, boxing was an important sport in our culture. It is a sport that, paradoxically, grew in popularity *and* in disfavor. Boxing, with its controlled violence, served as an outlet for the young country's aggressive nature. Yet, social ideologies and power structures constrained women from participating in historically male-dominated sports.

Women's boxing entered the twentieth century fighting public resistance. State athletic commissioners did not sanction women boxers and refused to issue them licenses because the sport was considered too dangerous for women. The Nevada State Athletic Commission, however, made history in 1975 by issuing the first female boxing license to Caroline Svendsen. In California, Pat Pineda was the first female boxer to be licensed, in 1976. Twenty years later, in New York, the Golden Gloves attracted twenty-two women competitors. The National Female Golden Gloves, in Chicago at the writing of this essay in 2005, was expected to attract many more competitors. And women's amateur boxing may be sanctioned, for the first time as an Olympic sport, for the 2012 Summer Olympics in London. However, International Olympic Committee (IOC) officials have said that if women's boxing is included, some of the men's boxing divisions must be eliminated. So already there is opposition by male boxers and boxing fans who do not want to see men's divisions eliminated.

Since 1997, with the inauguration of the U.S. Women's National Championship, hosted by USA Boxing and held in Augusta, Georgia, women's amateur boxing competitions have been held in Europe, Africa, and Asia. In amateur boxing, USA Boxing is the national governing body for Olympic-style boxing and is a member of the International Amateur Boxing Association (IABA).

Some female amateur boxers have become professionals, including Trina "Iron Butterfly" Ortegon, who won a bronze medal in the first

2005 Albuquerque, New Mexico
Christy Martin training at the Jack Candelaria Community Center

Women's National Championships in Augusta and became a professional boxer in 1997. And in 2002, Stephanie "Golden Girl" Jaramillo, a competitor in the second Nationals, in 1998, in Anaheim, California, made her professional debut. Both women, who live in Albuquerque, New Mexico, have raised the standards for female boxing.

The first Women's World Boxing Championship was held in Scranton, Pennsylvania, in 2001. Podolsk, Russia, was to host the 2005 amateur competition. In France, in 2001, the all-European women's boxing championship took place. Egypt, India and Kazakhstan are among 28 countries represented in women's boxing organizations.

Women's perseverance and social movements that have changed American life have enabled women's boxing to survive despite years of being marginalized. World War II created opportunities for women to do men's work; the civil rights movement enabled women and disenfranchised populations to participate in greater numbers in previously prohibited social, political, and cultural activities; and the feminist movement and Title IX specifically gave women the right to participate in sports that had banned them. Moreover, women used the courts to gain the right to participate in boxing, opening the ring to more women. USA Boxing lifted its ban against women's boxing in 1993, after Dallas Malloy, a sixteen-year-old boxer from Bellingham, Washington, filed a lawsuit against that organization. More than 2,000 young women now belong to USA Boxing and compete in eleven weight classes of Olympic-style boxing.

Women's boxing intersects race, class, gender, and ethnicity in American culture and society. Chicanas, Anglos, Latinas, African Americans, Asian Americans, and Native Americans in female boxing come from diverse socioeconomic levels. Some are teachers, professors, and social workers. Others are military reservists, bank tellers, and bus drivers.

Women boxers fight because they can. They are confident in their skills, strength, and desire to enter the ring. Their willingness to break social barriers and—for some even to confront discrimination because of their sexual orientation—only strengthens their determination.

Boxing in some barrios has a long male history with families that have generations of boxers: grandfathers, fathers, uncles, brothers, and cousins. But the current generation of women fighters has no family history of boxing mothers and grandmothers. In some families, however, a woman gets into boxing because a brother or a father is a trainer or a boxer. Delia "Chikita" González, a former Womens International Boxing Federation (WIBF) world champion from Chamberino, New Mexico, was fortunate to have two boxing brothers and a boxing sister. Chikita began her boxing career when her father, a former amateur boxer, took her along when she was only eleven years old to

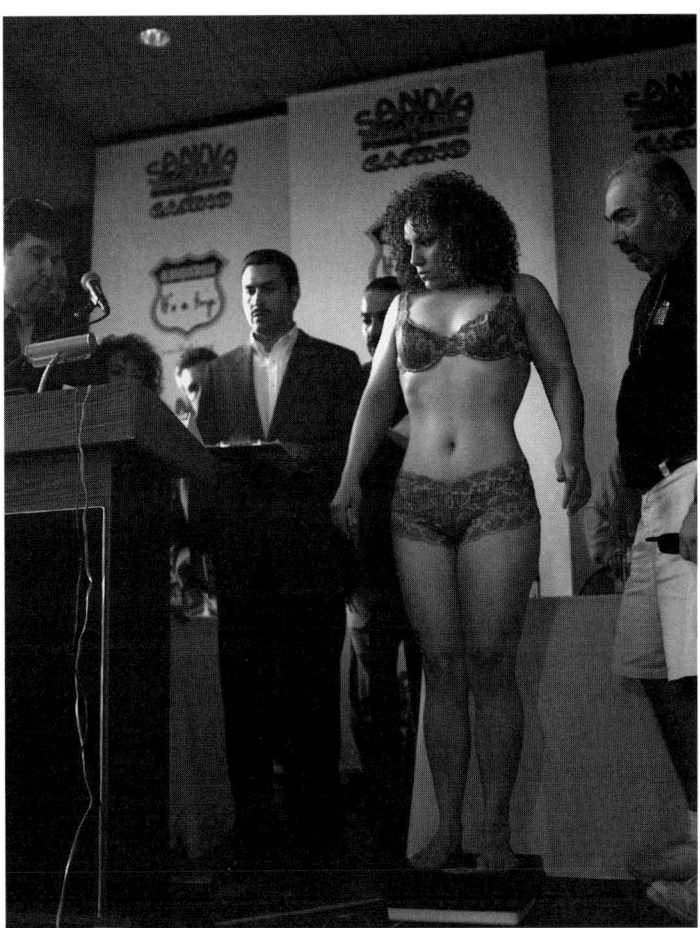

2003 Sandia Casino, Albuquerque, New Mexico
Stephanie Jaramillo weighs in

a gym that did not allow women. The sign, "NO FEMALES ALLOWED," came down the next day. Top-ranked Terri Cruz's boxing family includes her father and a brother who were professional boxers, a sister who is also a professional boxer, and two brothers who were champions in the Golden Gloves. Jackie Chávez, International Female Boxers Association (IFBA) Super Bantamweight Champion, started training with her uncle, Ray Sánchez II, who comes from an Albuquerque family of boxers.

II

In the world of boxing, women are subject to the "male gaze" in two of its forms.

Ring girls draw the leering male gaze as they sit ringside waiting to climb up to announce the rounds. Once in the ring, the girls sexily strut, in very high heels, as they hold up large cards. Their skimpy attire contributes to their characterization as "candy for the eye." The girls willingly pose for friends, photographers, and fans. Hoots and howls of derision that male fans direct at the ring girls devalue the seriousness of the women's boxing bouts. The long history of allegations that women boxers are women of ill-repute still hangs over the ring girls, although many of them are perfectly respectable mothers and wives.

Male fans do take the instinctive, primal fight for survival between women boxers more seriously than the precarious sashaying of the ring girls. But women fighters also attract the admiring male gaze. Fans see their strong bodies as evidence of toughness and intense, vigorous work. It is obvious to the men that without commitment, strenuous work, and long hours of training, these women would not be in voluntary combat for physical and strategic domination.

Much is read into the act of fighting. Homoeroticism runs strong in men's boxing, but is also perceived in women's boxing. The inherent drama of women in shorts and sports bras pulverizing and bloodying each other intensely arouses the crowds. That arousal is fueled further by having the trainers pour water over the women's heads and inside their shorts to help them cool down and rubbing and massaging their sweaty, muscled shoulders, arms, and thighs. This delivers a vicarious sensual experience for many of the male fans.

Boxing in the popular imagination historically has been obsessed with the white male body as a symbol of American values, ideals, and civilization. Women in boxing can be seen as a threat to "natural" male domination. Women's boxing triggers white male anxieties about social change.

The freedom to develop a sense of power is a political act in a world that still views male dominance not only as a prerogative that should

2005 Isleta Casino, Albuquerque, New Mexico
Crowd waits for main event, Holly Holm vs. Christy Martin

remain unchallenged but as a prerogative often associated with moral superiority. Sport, especially boxing, engenders differences between men and women. Boxing, for men, is a sport that cultivates force and skill, which makes men appear naturally powerful. As in many male-dominated sports, masculinity forces the subordination of women's physicality. Women have disrupted the highly structured sport of boxing by resisting ritualized, hegemonic masculinity. Women boxers symbolize and embody both feminist and masculine realities, surmounting the barriers of traditional femininity.

Sport, especially boxing, is a highly enhanced form of social realism in which aggression is associated with masculinity. Boxing entails strong physicality, including the clutching and embracing of hot, sweaty bodies. The body becomes

2003 Sandia Casino, Albuquerque, New Mexico
Ring Girl; Melissa Borzachillo

a weapon of domination. Boxing, "masculine" and violent, sneers at any evidence of weakness or femininity.

The female boxer becomes a subject of curiosity beyond the boxing event; she is watched, even her non-pugilistic behavior draws public attention. Attractive, beautiful boxers are asked why they risk getting hurt and disfigured—a question never asked of male fighters. One prominent promoter remains dead set against women's boxing, claiming it is repulsive and disgusting because he does not like to see women get battered. He has promoted women's boxing only under coercion. (Essentially: "Put women boxers on the card or the deal is off.") With the growing interest in women's boxing, however, trainers, managers, and promoters have become more supportive.

Women's boxing is still in its infancy. There are not enough fighters in the various weight divisions to produce compatible bouts, which is often a cause of mismatches. Women prizefighters struggle to get televised matches and appropriate prize money, even though women boxers are more exciting fighters and crowd pleasers than male fighters because they throw more punches and clinch less.

In boxing, the rhythm of the ring resembles ballet. Boxers are like dancers, using their bodies to express feelings, knowledge, and creativity. For example, Holly Holm, an International Boxing Association (IBA) junior welterweight champion, overcame her status as an underdog in a major non-title bout by dancing her way to victory with the constant motion of her footwork. She would move in, strike, and move away. Her body was attuned to her opponent's frustrations. Her dancing footwork delivered the message that Holm was strong and able to endure the few blows her opponent might manage to land.

Women's boxing is changing the nature of all boxing. In American society, lower status men sought to improve their lives through boxing. Boxing helped integrate new male immigrants into American society. With their strong, attractive bodies, these men became role models for members of the underclass. Many women boxers, however, are already well-established in their chosen careers or jobs. They become different sorts of role models. They let young women know that boxing can help them gain confidence, be aggressive, and be secure in their sexual orientation.

For example, Terri Cruz and Elisha Olivas are role-model mothers and yet they are fierce fighters when they are in the ring. Cruz, one of the top-ranked women in the world as a professional boxer, is saving to purchase a business in Denver, Colorado, her hometown, to continue to provide for her son and extended family after her boxing days are over. Olivas, a super featherweight also from Denver, disciplines her children firmly, but gently, and with love because she wants them to grow up well-behaved. To be a female boxer does not conflict with motherhood, femininity, or nurturing, nor is it evidence of or a cause of abnormality. Cruz and Olivas and the many other women boxers demonstrate to the boxing world that women are contributing to a sport that needs a new infusion of excitement. They are not inferior, not weak, not unnatural athletes, and not unnatural females.

2005 Houston, Texas
Yolanda Swindell at Prince Boxing Gym

Women boxers demand a greater role in the ring for themselves and other women. They see boxing as a legitimate context in which to establish a sense of identity. They feel free to challenge the social expectations of the "natural" way women must care for others. Women's boxing is growing, both as a form of fitness-program exercise and as a sport, due to attention from the mass media and fans. More and more young women are taking up boxing as amateurs, often with the goal of participating in the Golden Gloves and the Olympic Games. Perhaps the young women are not aware of society's resistance to females in boxing and other male dominated sports. Nevertheless, they are challenging society's sense of femininity *and* masculinity.

Boxing is a sport that depends on the use of violence. Boxers use their bodies as weapons to win by inflicting pain and injury and, at times, unfortunately, death. Women boxers, just as male boxers, are willing to pay the personal cost of participating in such a brutal and violent sport. Females take just as much pride as men in establishing their reputations in a sport that can bring great injury.

III

Social ideologies strengthen and legitimatize class and ethnic inequalities in sports while at the same time offering an arena in which prejudices can be challenged.

Homophobia in society and sports enforces conformity through gender-role control. Nontraditional behavior is feared and disdained by homophobes. Homophobia hurts female boxers who may be lesbian and are often viewed as women acting like men. Homophobia maintains gender stereotypes and attempts to regulate sexual behavior.

Lesbian athletes are subjected to stigmatization and discrimination, both overt and subtle. They represent a serious challenge to male dominance and traditional sexual behavior. Lesbian boxers often are considered to have less to lose than male-homosexual sports participants by openly revealing their sexual orientation. And once they actually begin fighting, their "masculine" behavior is more easily tolerated by men who highly value strength and physical prowess. Lesbian boxers upset the dominant perception of heterosexuality in sports, although they may face more obstacles than other women boxers.

Women's boxing, like men's boxing, is governed by sanctioning bodies that form policies, rules, and regulations to ensure the safety of the boxers. The groups' goal is to bring integrity to women's boxing. Governing organizations and amateur competitions have formed a self-contained system, but with connections to an expanding network, including promoters, managers, and trainers. Women's boxing, also like men's boxing, creates jobs: trainers, promoters, and managers. A small number of those jobs are now going to women. (Note: in other sports commandeered by women the jobs usually go to *men*.) Women are judges, doctors, corner people, and a few are referees. Trina Ortegon, a former IFBA world super-middleweight and IBA middleweight champion, is now a member of the New Mexico State Athletic Commission. She retired from the ring after a shoulder injury that required long-term medical attention.

The International Women's Boxing Federation (IWBF), formed in 1992, issued

2003 Sky Ute Casino, Ignacio, Colorado
Teri "Lil' Loca" Lynn Cruz

a series of rules to be followed by boxing commissions in the United States and the world. The IWBF commissioners monitor rankings of the professional women boxers, and attempt to ensure compliance with the federation's rules:

> Ten rounds, instead of the usual 12 of men's boxing, for all world title fights.
>
> Two-minute rounds, not the three-minute rounds in regular men's boxing.
>
> The use of 8-oz. gloves for competitors who weigh up to 140 pounds and 10-oz. gloves for those who weigh more.
>
> Women must have medical examinations.

> Boxers must be licensed to fight.
>
> Pregnancy tests are required for all women before matches.
>
> Titles must be defended within a reasonable time to allow the remaining competitors in the respective weight divisions a chance to win the titles.

Some women, though, consider the differences between women's and men's boxing regulations to be patronizing.

Formed in 1997, the International Female Boxers Association (IFBA) also promotes women's professional boxing throughout the world. Additionally, IFBA supports the induction of women into the Boxing Hall of Fame.

Women's boxing still lags behind men's boxing in skill levels, due to its marginal status, but women boxers will catch up with time. Sandy Martínez-Pino, a longtime state, national, and international amateur boxing official from Albuquerque, is convinced that as more amateur boxers move up to become professionals, women's boxing will be taken more seriously.

With Title IX, passed in 1972, women's participation in all levels of sport has increased. However, coverage of women's sports is less than that given to men's sports. Promoters often claim that women's boxing, to be marketed in the profit-driven market, must have "sex appeal."

At times, it takes monstrous actions to change social practices that have been accepted as "natural." All-women boxing series, featuring accomplished and emerging women fighters of various ethnicities are becoming popular with the fans. Films such as "Knockout," "Million Dollar Baby," "Girl Fight," and the documentary "Shadow Boxers," and books such as *Reach, Without Apology, Looking for a Fight*, and *The Boxer's Heart* are helping to popularize women's boxing.

Christy "Coal Miner's Daughter" Martin is credited with rekindling major interest in modern professional women's boxing. Unfortunately, she has vehemently refused to be an advocate for women's boxing. Lucia Rijker, whose amazing boxing career is documented in "Shadow Boxers," had a role in the movie, "Million Dollar Baby." Mia Rosales-St. John, best remembered for her pose on the front cover of *Playboy*, has been knocking out opponents since 1997. Ann Wolfe has

earned several world titles as a junior middleweight (IFBA, WIBC), super middleweight (IBFA, WIBC), and light heavyweight (IBA). Valerie Mahfood has won IWBF and WIBF light heavyweight world titles and is a former super middleweight champion of the world.

The boxing daughters of famous male boxers include: Laila Ali, daughter of the great Mohammad Ali; J'Marie Moore, Archie Moore's youngest daughter; Jacqueline Frazier-Lynde, Joe Frazier's daughter (a lawyer turned professional boxer); Irichelle Durán, the daughter of Roberto Durán; and Freeda Foreman, George Foreman's daughter.

In some regions, particularly the Southwest, women's boxing is very popular, and fighters with growing fan bases include Jackie Chávez, IFBA super bantamweight champion, who loves to skydive; Mónica Lovato, a competitive junior bantamweight; Stephanie "Golden Girl" Jaramillo, a junior welterweight now retired who has turned promoter; and Holly Holm, an IBA junior welterweight champion. All are from New Mexico.

IV

Several years ago, I finally got the courage to visit A Woman's Place Boxing Gym and was immediately impressed by owner Irene García and the women who were training. As I soon learned, García did not cut any slack for her charges, regardless of fitness levels or age. She was disciplined and rigorous in her training program. The first time I sparred was traumatic; being hit in the head was an experience I had never had—and never want to have again. I got angry, lost control, became aggressive, and started whaling away at my opponent. After that display, my boxing colleagues were warned to be wary that despite my age I was dangerous. I was a member of the gym until García closed it in 2001. After weeks of missing my boxing exercise program, I visited the Jake Candelaria Community Center that is also a local boxing gym in one of the roughest neighborhoods of Albuquerque. The gym is known for producing accomplished male amateur and professional boxers. In the beginning, none of the men—trainers, managers, or boxers—would talk to me. No one approached me for several weeks, although I was very aware that my boxing skills were being observed. Finally, one of the boxers whose curiosity was greater than his reserve, commented on my skills and said I had good form. It was at that moment that I knew I was accepted and being taken seriously, rather than thought of as merely someone seeking male companionship. One practice that

2005 Albuquerque, New Mexico
Jackie Chávez with trainer Sergio Chávez

I had to learn to overlook was all the spitting. In boxing gyms, plastic covered containers are placed where boxers can easily spit into them. Whenever I noticed boxers spitting, I had to struggle to keep my stomach from wrenching. Another thing I had to learn was to leave my feminism outside the gym doors. I could not reproach the men for

Referring to women as girls

Making comments about my body

Prying into my marital status

Boxing as an exercise program has been the most satisfying of any that I have tried. Boxing is terrific for expending anger and frustration. Whenever I am angry, I picture the faces of those with whom I am furious and punch the bags as hard as I can. In those moments *I am monstrous*, not a demure, quiet, woman.

Yes, women boxers are *monstrous*! But only for breaking the bonds and stereotypes that have oppressed women in sports, especially in boxing.

Boxing is a rougher world than the academic world at the University of New Mexico, where I am a faculty member and senior reference librarian in the Center for Southwest Research. Yet I have met wonderful, dedicated, and gentle people in the boxing gym.

On one occasion, I mentioned to University of Houston art professor and photographer, Delilah Montoya, that I was working on Chicana/Latina boxers, a research subject that has not received attention. Delilah asked if she could work with me, and we soon were covering boxing matches together in New Mexico, Texas, and Colorado. I even covered a bout in White Plains, New York, when Victoria Cisneros, an Albuquerque native, fought Ann Marie Succarato, a more-experienced light welterweight, in the first women's professional bout in the Westchester County Center.

Delilah quickly developed an appreciation for the "sweet science." Photographing subjects in constant motion is not easy, but Delilah caught some memorable flashes of the boxing world, capturing artistic images of managers, trainers, promoters, ring girls, and fans as well as the female fighters. It has indeed been a pleasure and a learning experience to work with Delilah Montoya, an accomplished competitor in her own profession.

BIBLIOGRAPHY
Books

Ali, Laila. *Finding Strength, Spirit, and Personal Power.* New York: Hyperion Books, 2003.

Cohen, Leah Hager. *Without Apology: Girls, Women, and the Desire to Fight.* New York: Random House, 2005.

Denfeld, Rene. *Kill the Body, the Head will Fall.* New York: Warner, 1997.

Guttmann, Allen. *Women's Sports: A History.* New York: Columbia University Press, 1991.

Halber, Christy. *Understanding the Sports and Skills. of Boxing.* Brentwood, TN: ISI Publishing, 2003.

Picket, Lynn Snowden. *Looking for a Fight: a Memoir.* New York: The Dial Press, 2000.

Oates, Joyce Carol. *On Boxing.* New York: Dolphin, 1987.

Rotella, Carlo. *Good with Their Hands: Boxers, Bluesmen and Other Characters from the Rust Belt.* 2004. (Includes women boxers and ring girls.)

Sekules, Kate. *The Boxer's Heart: How I Fell in Love with the Ring.* New York: Villard, 2000.

Films

"Eye of the Tiger" (working title) will chronicle the lives of four amateur female boxers. Forthcoming.

"Girl Fight." Director: Karyn Kusama, 2000.

"Knockout." Director: Lorenzo Doumani, 2000.

"Million Dollar Baby." Director: Clint Eastwood, 2004.

"Shadow Boxers." Director: Katya Bankowsky, 2003.

Internet Sources

Women's Boxing Archive Network (WBAN)

RPM Boxing

Fight News: Inside Women's Boxing

María Teresa Márquez is an associate professor and University of New Mexico Regents Lecturer and curator of the Chicano, Hispano, and Latino Library Research Program.

Women Boxers
The New Warriors

Delilah Montoya, University of Houston

The boxers in this book represent a new generation of women who grew up with such role models as Wonder Woman, the PowerPuff Girls, Cat Woman and, in some cases, working mothers. However, my interest is in thinking about them as *malcriadas*. My interpretation of a *malcriada* is that of an "ill-mannered servant" or "bad girl." A *malcriada* is a woman who will not behave and is determined to do what she wants, regardless of what society rules or even good sense dictates. When a family is confronted with this sort of unseemly member, they struggle to change her. Welcoming the uphill battle, the *malcriada* remains unchanged; in the end, the family learns to accept her and even become proud of her accomplishments.

Women boxers certainly fit the definition of *malcriada*. By crossing the ropes and getting into the ring, they enter into the bastions of manliness to confront a brutal sport. A social understanding has always been that a woman is not to witness, demonstrate, or indulge in acts of violence. Many, in fact, are appalled by the violent sport of boxing and say that it should be banned. But the *malcriadas*, determined to box, turn their backs on these opinions. Title IX of the Civil Rights Act and the feminist movement gave women the right, and they willingly have taken it.

The inspiration to push limits and break barriers is as varied as the boxers themselves. At the young age of five, Stephanie Jaramillo was inspired by Mike Tyson; watching his moves on TV fueled her desire to control the ring. Mónica Lovato points to the tragic death of her boyfriend; boxing helps her remember him by connecting to his fighting nature. He was a street fighter who gained the respect of the Espanola community in New Mexico. Fighting and winning give her that same respect.

2005 Houston, Texas
*Brajae Joyner with her sister Kyandrea Joyner
at Progressive Amateur Boxing Association*

Pueblo Boxing Gym; *Karen García,* Top Ten Boxing Gym; *Crystal Delgado and Mónica Flores,* Ray Sánchez's Boxing Gym; *a mixed match,* Top Ten Boxing Gym; *Mónica Flores*

Some of these women were kick boxers who stopped kicking and started boxing because of the lack of fights in the kickboxing sport. Jodie Esquibel and Holly Holm were both kick boxers. They train with Mike Winkeljohn, a champion fighter who held three world titles (two Muay Thai belts and one kickboxing belt) during his professional career. Believing Jodie's and Holly's talents would take them further as professional boxers, Mike coached them into making the switch. Holly holds an IBA Light Welterweight Title and Jody's speed in the ring makes her a commanding contender. Jackie Chávez, whose talent earned an IFBA Super Bantamweight Title, has a similar story. Her trainer, Sergio Chávez, fought for sixteen years as an amateur fighter and, to date, he has coached professionally for fifteen years. He teaches Jackie her boxing skills. Once a kick boxer, Jackie now faces her opponents as a professional female fighter.

Professional boxing is an established combat sport, at least for men, and provides women the rare opportunity to be professional athletes. Akondaye is a seasoned athlete whose goals are to win a belt while obtaining a Ph.D. in Clinical Psychology. By boxing, she can sustain a career as a professional athlete. Her athletic career started with junior high school track and basketball. In college at Texas Southern University she was on the track team and after graduation she turned to fitness competitions. In 2005, she is the number one Light Middleweight female boxer on the WBAN chart. Akondaye has won many of her bouts with technical knockouts.

2005 Houston, Texas
Samantha and Christian Galván with Crystal Martínez and Diana Martínez at Ray's Boxing Club

Like Mohammed Ali's daughter Laila, Terri Cruz grew up in a boxing family; her father and brothers were professional prizefighters. However, at the age of eighteen, Terri became a single mother. Single mothers who box professionally are common in the sport. Lucy Contreras, Doreen Hilton, and Elisha Olivas are also single mothers who use the purses they earn to provide for their young families.

Very few women boxers can afford to work exclusively on their boxing careers; most balance this interest with other jobs. They work as waitresses, security guards, medical or social workers, office workers, or are full-time students. In general, female boxers come from working-class families that teach them that determination and hard work are instrumental in achieving their goals. Yolanda Swindell, like all the other boxers, trains five days a week to build her body and mind for the good fight. To do anything less could yield injuries while fighting in the ring. For the boxer, this is the devil that waits in her corner.

Now for the first time, in 2012, boxing will bring in Olympic gold for amateur female boxers. And many of the non-profit boxing gyms that train the amateur fighters are preparing their young women for this challenge. This is a pivotal moment for the boxing community.

Las Malcriadas' Profiles

2005 Albuquerque, New Mexico
Holly Holm with her IBA Junior Welterweight Belt

1

Super Flyweight

24

Mónica Lovato

Pound for pound, Mónica holds her own ground and proves to be an overwhelming adversary to anyone she fights. While photographing Mónica's portrait, I complained to her that it is hard to snap a good fight shot when she knocks her opponent down within 48 seconds of the first round. She responded, "I don't know why she didn't get up. I would have."

Mónica Lovato
vs
Nancy Bonilla

June 12, 2005
Ohkay Casino, San Juan Pueblo, NM, USA
Fire Inside Productions, Ross Sánchez

Mónica Lovato	Boxer	Nancy Bonilla
US American	**Nationality**	Puerto Rican
Albuquerque, NM, USA	**Hometown**	Camuy, Puerto Rico
Super Flyweight	**Rated at**	Flyweight
7/39	**World Rank**	31/51
Southpaw	**Stance**	Orthodox
5' 5"	**Height**	5' 1"
28	**Age**	33
Al Lovato	**Trainer**	Jomar Pérez
	Pro Bouts	
3 (1 KOs)	**Wins**	2 (1 KO)
1	**Losses**	3
0	**Draws**	0
4	**Total**	5

The hometown crowd went wild as Mónica Lovato knocked out Nancy Bonilla in the first 48 seconds of a four-round bout.

Super Flyweight

Jodie Esquibel

Jodie has a small stature, yet she prefers to spar with boxers who are taller and outweigh her. She believes this gives her an advantage when fighting those in her own weight class. Her first professional bout ended in the second round at 1:39 with a technical knockout win. Jodie does not take losing lightly, two of her four amateur losses were avenged.

Jodie Esquibel
vs
Doreen Hilton

June 24, 2005
Isleta Casino, Albuquerque, NM, USA
Fresquez Productions Inc., Lenny Fresquez

Jodie Esquibel	Boxer	Doreen Hilton
US American	**Nationality**	US American
Albuquerque, NM, USA	**Hometown**	Denver, CO, USA
Super Flyweight	**Rated at**	Super Flyweight
Professional Debut 6-24-05	**World Rank**	36/39
Orthodox	**Stance**	Orthodox
5' 1"	**Height**	5'
19	**Age**	25
Mike Winkeljohn	**Trainer**	Steve Maestas
	Pro Bouts	
0 (0 KOs)	**Wins**	0 (0 KOs)
0	**Losses**	3
0	**Draws**	0
0	**Total**	3

When Jodie knocked down Doreen for the third time, she won her professional debut with a 1:39 technical knockout in the second round.

3
Bantamweight

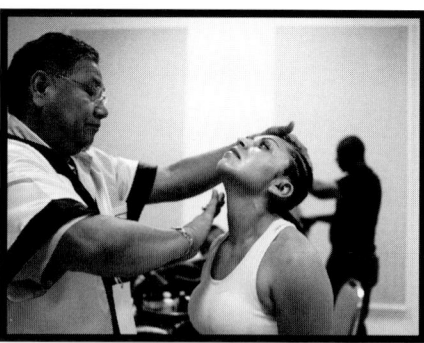

María Lucy Contreras

Training was a weight loss program for Lucy Contreras, but more than that it has provided her with a community. Her trainer, Ray Ontiveros, owns Ray's Boxing Club and also manages her boxing career; in turn she helps him with the club's daily operations. This gives Lucy a sense of accomplishment. Not only do powerful athletes emerge from the club but also a community gets built. Many of the wards, or precincts, in Houston, like many other cities, host their own boxing clubs and gyms.

María Lucy Contreras
vs
Valeria "Leoncita" Flores

March 30, 2005
Civic Center, New Braunfels, TX, USA
Bam Bam Promotions

María Lucy Contreras	Boxer	Valeria Flores
US American	**Nationality**	US American
Houston, TX, USA	**Hometown**	San Antonio, TX, USA
Bantamweight	**Rated at**	Featherweight
30/65	**World Rank**	16/67
Orthodox	**Stance**	Orthodox
5' 1"	**Height**	5' 4"
30	**Age**	32
Ramón "Ray" Ontiveros, Sr.	**Trainer**	Eldimiro Dávila
	Pro Bouts	
1 (0 KOs)	**Wins**	5 (0 KOs)
0	**Losses**	2
0	**Draws**	0
1	**Total**	7

After exchanging blows for four rounds with "Leoncita", Lucy lost by a split decision. Judge David Harris 36-40, Judge Rick Crocker 37-39, Judge Perry Hillin 39-37.

4
Super Bantamweight

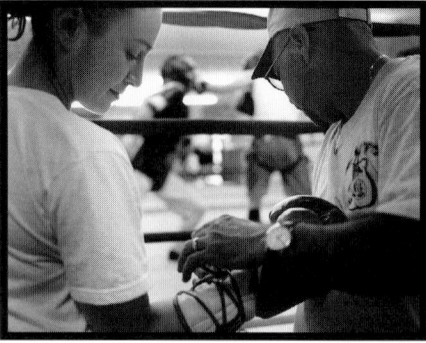

Jackie Chávez

I asked Jackie, "If you could fight anyone, who would that be?" After a thoughtful moment, she said, "Audrey Vela. I would like to fight her again."

Jackie's childhood dream was to fly, to be a pilot. Skydiving is the closest she has come to fulfilling that vision. Jackie claims she feels free and tranquil and compares the rush of adrenaline to winning a fight. Although Jackie has been successful in her boxing career, she intends to become a physical therapist. While both her grandmother and mother support her boxing, they will be even more pleased with her future career. Jackie credits her sister for keeping her balanced in boxing, work, and life.

Jackie holds the IFBA Super Bantamweight Title. According to the September 9, 2005, ratings on the www.insidewomensboxing.com website, Jackie is ranked in the top 5 of the WBC, WIBA and WBAN charts.

Jackie Chávez
vs
Audrey Vela

June 12, 2005
Ohkay Casino, San Juan Pueblo, NM, USA
Fire Inside Productions, Ross Sánchez

Jackie Chávez	Boxer	Audrey Vela
US American	Nationality	US American
Los Chavez, NM, USA	Hometown	Austin, TX, USA
Super Bantamweight	Rated at	Bantamweight
10/43	World Rank	15/62
Orthodox	Stance	Orthodox
5' 3"	Height	5' 3"
22	Age	24
Sergio Chávez	Trainer	Rudy Vásquez
	Pro Bouts	
8 (3 KOs)	Wins	6 (1 KOs)
0	Losses	1
0	Draws	0
8	Total	7

For ten rounds both boxers fought fiercely, but Jackie Chávez kept her title by capturing the best side of a split decision. Judge James Bagshaw 97-93, Judge Larry Chávez 97-94, Judge Levi Martínez 93-97.

5
Super Bantamweight

Terri "Lil' Loca" Lynn Cruz

Terri Cruz, IFBA Bantamweight Champion, has been boxing professionally for six years. Her first fight was with Elisha Olivas on June 6, 1999. Yet, Terri looks beyond her boxing career and has started a professional cleaning business with her sister as a way of providing for her three children. Continuing with the boxing family tradition, Steve Maestas, her trainer and manager, is the father of her youngest daughter, Genesis Stevie Lynn. When asked if she would encourage her children to box, Teri responded, "Ya, I'll work their corner."

Terri "Lil' Loca" Lynn Cruz
vs
Jessica "Goodnite" Mohs

October, 10, 2003
Sky Ute Casino, Ignacio, CO, USA
Sky Ute Promotions, Ben Fernández

Terri Lynn Cruz	Boxer	Jessica Mohs
US American	**Nationality**	US American
Denver, CO, USA	**Hometown**	Phoenix, AZ, USA
Super Bantamweight	**Rated at**	Lightweight
7/43	**World Rank**	25/50
Orthodox	**Stance**	Orthodox
5' 3 ½"	**Height**	5' 3"
32	**Age**	30
Steve Maestas	**Trainer**	Clement Vierra
	Pro Bouts	
11 (7 KOs)	**Wins**	5 (1 KOs)
4	**Losses**	11
2	**Draws**	1
17	**Total**	17

Terri Cruz won by a Split Decision in a six round bout by simply out boxing Jessica "Goodnite" Mohs.

6

Super Featherweight

Elisha Olivas

"Boxing keeps me serene...," Elisha Olivas said when interviewed by Master Sgt. Cheryl L. Toner of the 380th Air Expeditionary Wing Public Affairs Department for the *Sand Script Expeditionary Edition*. "Everything goes blank. I watch her moves, I watch myself, and when I smell blood, I go for the kill." Elisha is describing the "zone," the place from which the fighter operates while in the heat of battle. She learned about survival as a child with the death of her father and then by watching her mother attempt to keep the family together. All the while, Elisha set out on a spiritual search by preparing herself to become a nun. The dots mysteriously crossed and then reconnected and she found self-determination in the ring.

Shortly after her bout with Elizabeth "Pink Panther" Monge, Elisha, who is also a senior airman reservist, left for a six-month deployment in Southwest Asia from Peterson Air Force Base, Colorado.

Elisha Olivas
vs
Elizabeth "Pink Panther" Monge

October, 10, 2003
Sky Ute Casino, Ignacio, CO, USA
Sky Ute Promotions, Ben Fernández

Elisha Olivas	Boxer	Elizabeth Monge
US American	Nationality	US American
Denver, CO, USA	Hometown	Farmington, NM, USA
Super Featherweight	Rated at	Light Flyweight
23/50	World Rank	Professional Debut 10-3-03
Orthodox	Stance	Orthodox
5' 2"	Height	5' 3"
27	Age	19
Steve Maestas	Trainer	Horacio Monge
	Pro Bouts	
1 (1 KOs)	Wins	0 (0 KOs)
4	Losses	0
1	Draws	0
6	Total	0

Elisha received the wining end of a mixed decision after going four rounds with Elizabeth "Pink Panther" Monge.

7
Lightweight

Mia "The Knockout" St. John

Mia Rosales St. John, a celebrity female boxer, is an accomplished athlete in Tae Kwon Do and a Female Boxing Champion. She holds the IBA Women's Lightweight Title and the IFBA Lightweight World Title. Mia's boxing career spans nearly a decade, beginning on Valentine's Day, 1997, when she delivered a 54-second KO and received her alias, "The Knockout."

In many ways, celebrity boxers recreate their identity and by extension their communities' identities as they enter the ring. By becoming Mohammed Ali, Cassius Clay promoted a Black Power agenda; Corky Gonzales through his efforts to box in Colorado promoted a Chicano one. Mia Rosales St. John up-ended the politics of identity by blurring the boundaries between the champion feminist athlete and the foxy boxer. In 1999, St. John appeared on the cover of *Playboy*. The message she sent was that the woman athlete does not leave behind her sensuality; rather it is always part of her female self. The identity she created hosts a self-confident sexuality with a powerful athletic fortitude, a construct that clearly hits home for the post-feminist woman.

Mia has not forgotten her Mexican heritage or her mother's inspirational words: "*El saber es poder*/Knowledge is power." By using her celebrity status, Mia has set up a foundation, "El Saber Es Poder," to assist the education of children living in migrant camps throughout the United States.

Mia "The Knockout" St. John
vs
Liz Drew

June 12, 2005
Ohkay Casino, San Juan Pueblo, NM, USA
Fire Inside Productions, Ross Sánchez

Mia St. John	Boxer	Liz Drew
US American	**Nationality**	US American
San Fernando Valley, CA, USA	**Hometown**	Troy, MO, USA
Lightweight	**Rated at**	Lightweight
12/39	**World Rank**	18/39
Orthodox	**Stance**	Orthodox
5' 6"	**Height**	5' 7"
38	**Age**	34
Roberto García	**Trainer**	Sam Gaines
	Pro Bouts	
40 (17 KOs)	**Wins**	9 (2 KOs)
5	**Losses**	7
2	**Draws**	0
47	**Total**	16

Mia Rosales St. John defeated Liz Drew in a ten-round match. She scored a unanimous decision and received the vacant IFBA Lightweight World Title.

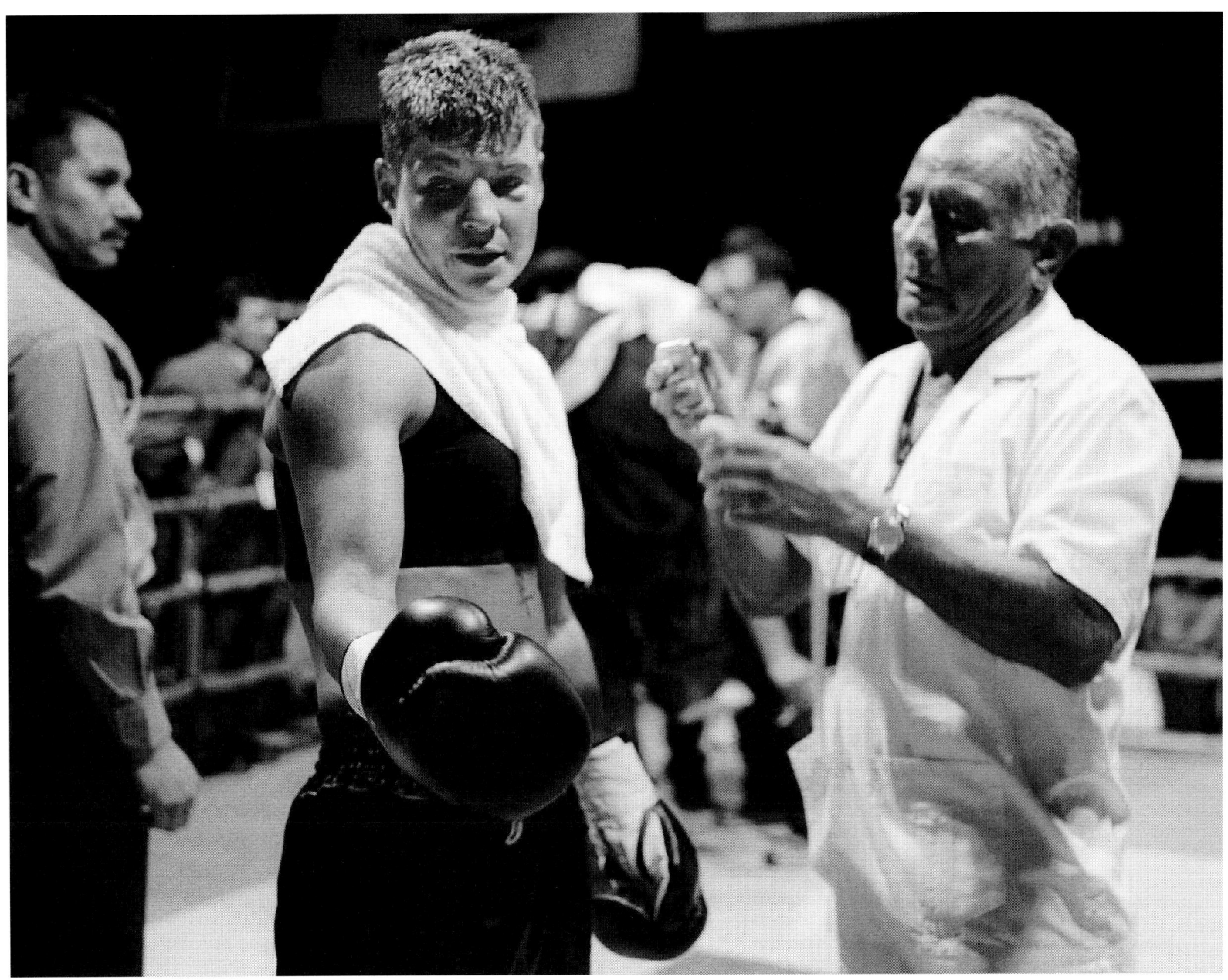

8
Light Welterweight

Stephanie "Golden Girl" Jaramillo

When Stephanie Jaramillo began boxing, she set out to achieve three goals: to fight the world's greatest, to be a champion, and to become a promoter. During her amateur career, Stephanie reigned as a number one boxer with 46 wins (18 by knockout), 3 losses, and 2 draws. After fighting a few professional matches, Stephanie became a top contender on the Women's International Boxing Federation and the Global Boxing Union charts.

With just a six-day notice, on December 3, 2004, in Kansas City in front of 7,000 people, Stephanie stepped into the ring with the fiercest female fighter in her weight class; Sumaya Anani. "Sumaya Anani was my idol, the best there was. Just fighting her, wining or losing, would fill my belly," said Stephanie about her last fight. The fight went ten rounds, during which Stephanie suffered a broken nose and lost by a unanimous decision. However, Stephanie's epiphany came when Anani punched to stop her heart, but instead it skipped a beat and opened her mind. Promoting is another obtainable goal; Stephanie is setting out to be a great one.

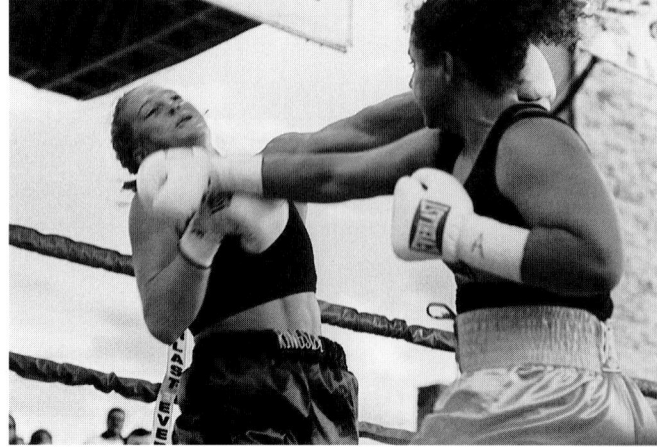

Stephanie "Golden Girl" Jaramillo
vs
Holly Holm

August 26, 2003
Sandia Casino, Albuquerque, NM, USA
Sugar Ray Leonard Boxing, Sugar Ray Leonard

Stephanie Jaramillo	Boxer	Holly Holm
US American	**Nationality**	US American
Albuquerque, NM, USA	**Hometown**	Albuquerque, NM, USA
Light Welterweight	**Rated at**	Light Welterweight
13/56	**World Rank**	15/56
Orthodox	**Stance**	Southpaw
5' 5"	**Height**	5' 8"
21	**Age**	21
Floyd Mayweather, Sr., Pat Holmes, Ricky & Rick Jaramillo	**Trainer**	Mike Winkeljohn
	Pro Bouts	
3 (2 KOs)	**Wins**	4 (2 KOs)
0	**Losses**	0
0	**Draws**	0
3	**Total**	4

After a four-round match, Stephanie suffered her first professional loss. She received a mixed decision that favored Holly Holm. Judge Tommy Pappas 38–38, Judge Levi Martínez 37–39, Judge William Gantt 37–40.

Stephanie "Golden Girl" Jaramillo
vs
Holly Holm

October 3, 2003
Sandia Casino, Albuquerque, NM, USA
Sugar Ray Leonard Boxing, Sugar Ray Leonard

Stephanie requited her August 26 loss to Holly with a six-round draw.

9
Light Welterweight

Holly Holm

Holly Holm received the IBA Junior Welterweight Belt. She is ranked in the top 5 on the WBC, WIBA and is number one on the WBAN chart in the October 2005 ratings.

On September 16, 2005, at the Isleta Casino, Holly Holm, became a "Million Dollar Baby" when she toppled the legendary Christy Martin by a unanimous decision. Holly, a minister's daughter, grew up in Los Lunas, New Mexico, a predominately Native American and Hispanic community. There she learned to gain respect, and certainly her success as a boxer has earned the respect of the New Mexico community.

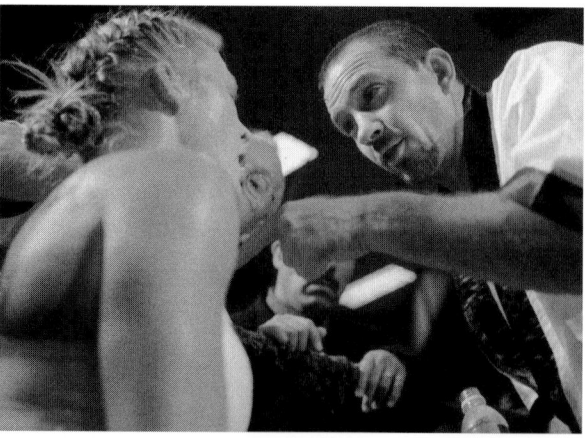

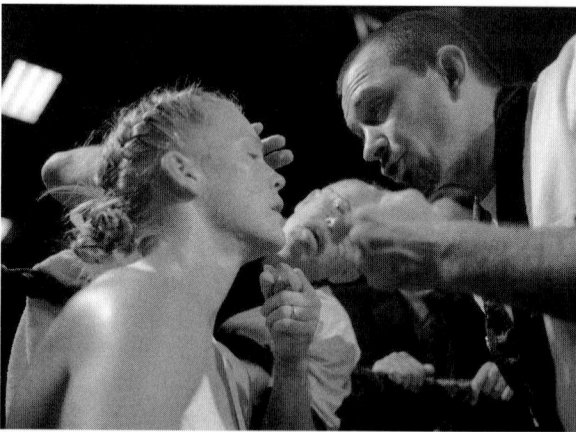

Holly Holm
vs
Lisa "Lil' Warrior" Lewis

June, 24, 2005
Isleta Casino, Albuquerque, NM, USA
Fresquez Productions Inc., Lenny Fresquez

Holly Holm	Boxer	Lisa Lewis
US American	**Nationality**	US American
Albuquerque, NM, USA	**Hometown**	Fresno, CA, USA
Light Welterweight	**Rated at**	Lightweight
7/56	**World Rank**	10/39
Southpaw	**Stance**	Orthodox
5' 8"	**Height**	5' 5"
23	**Age**	39
Mike Winkeljohn	**Trainer**	Wes Hodgins
	Pro Bouts	
9 (4 KOs)	**Wins**	7 (3 KOs)
1	**Losses**	12
2	**Draws**	0
12	**Total**	19

Fighting to maintain her IBA Light Welterweight Title, Holly won by technical knockout when Lisa Lewis failed to respond to the bell at the end of the eighth round of a ten-round match.

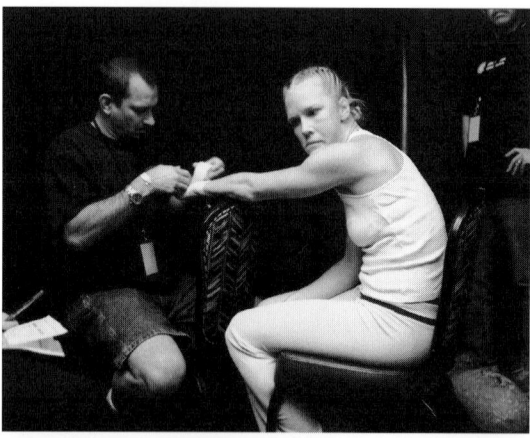

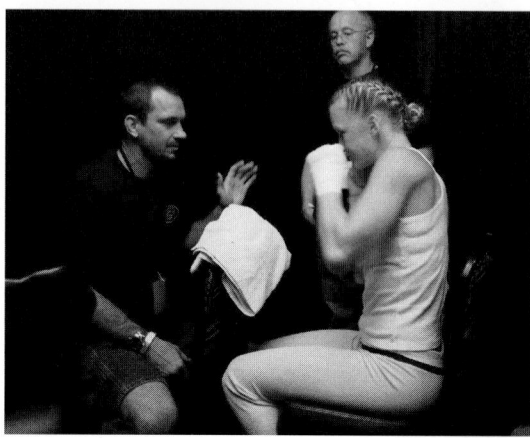

Holly Holm
vs
Christy "Coalminer's Daughter" Martin

September, 16, 2005
Isleta Casino, Albuquerque, NM, USA
Fresquez Productions Inc., Lenny Fresquez

Holly Holm	Boxer	Christy Martin
US American	**Nationality**	US American
Albuquerque, NM, USA	**Hometown**	Orlando, FL, USA
Light Welterweight	**Rated at**	Welterweight
3/56	**World Rank**	4/28
Southpaw	**Stance**	Orthodox
5' 8"	**Height**	5'4 ½"
23	**Age**	37
Mike Winkeljohn	**Trainer**	Jim Martin
	Pro Bouts	
10 (4 KOs)	**Wins**	46 (31 KOs)
1	**Losses**	3
2	**Draws**	2
13	**Total**	51

Despite being knocked down by Christy early in their ten-round bout, Holly sprang up and went on to win by an unanimous decision. At the end of the fight, Christy quickly left the ring while Holly bathed in her victory for the hometown crowd.

10
Welterweight

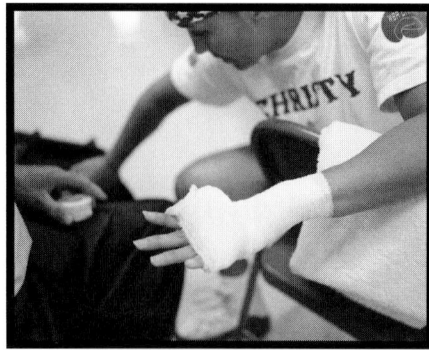

Christy "Coalminer's Daughter" Martin

"I started with nothing and had nothing for a long time. I struggled from the bottom up, year after year," Christy stated to Lori Steinhorst during her interview for the article, "Toe to Toe with Christy Martin." As Christy's boxing fame rose, she pulled female boxing along as a reputable sport. True to the sport, Christy understands herself as a boxer. She explained to Lori Steinhorst that she was not trying to make a statement as a woman or for women; rather she simply wanted to fight for the love of the sport. She asserted, "I'm a fighter."

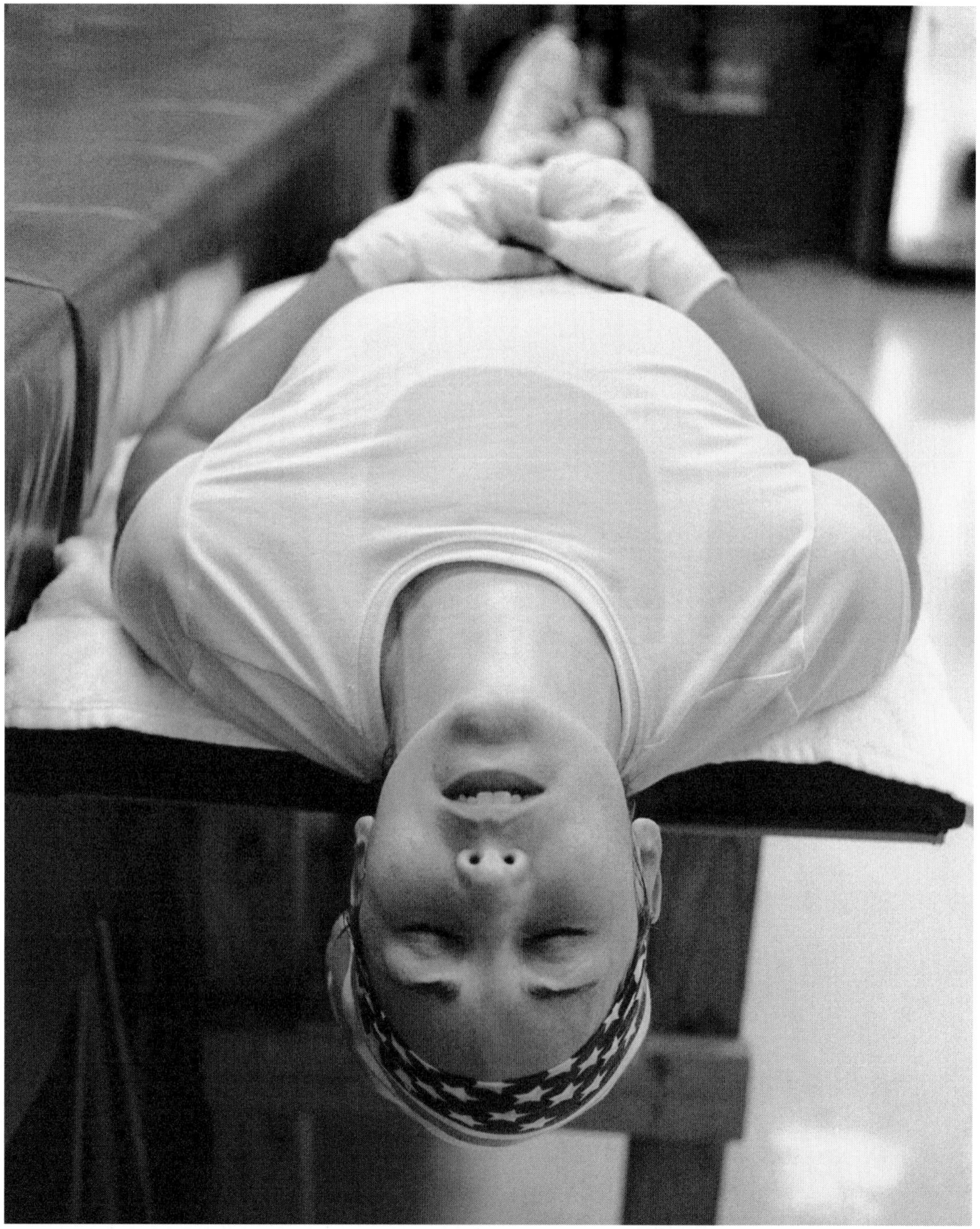

11

Light Middleweight

Akondaye "Storm" Fountain

Ranked number one on the September 2005 BoxRec.com world chart, Akondaye Fountain is a powerful boxer. She balances her growth as a mother, psycotherapist, and wife with athletic ambitions. Akondaye believes her love for family and God is her strongest asset. Usually training and sparring with men, she feels uneasy about fighting women; Akondaye said that she does not want to cripple her opponent. Learning this, I asked her how she found the drive to exchange blows. "Oh," she answered, "I just unleash my vicious side."

Akondaye "Storm" Fountain
vs
Krystle M. Davis

January, 21, 2005
Reliant Center, Houston, TX, USA
Miller Lite, Main Events & Texas Title Belts

Akondaye Fountain	Boxer	Krystle M. Davis
US American	**Nationality**	US American
Houston, TX, USA	**Hometown**	Odessa, TX, USA
Light Middleweight	**Rated at**	Light Heavyweight
3/26	**World Rank**	Professional Debut 1-21-05
Orthodox	**Stance**	Orthodox
5' 6"	**Height**	5' 10"
32	**Age**	21
Ronnie Shield, Hylon "Cedric" Williams	**Trainer**	Rudy Rodríquez, Fabián Núñez
	Pro Bouts	
3 (1 KOs)	**Wins**	0 (0 KOs)
0	**Losses**	0
0	**Draws**	0
3	**Total**	0

When the referee ended the fight, thirty-two seconds into the third round, Akondaye brought home another technical knockout.

12
Super Middleweight

Yolanda "Stone Hands" Swindell

"The difference between a woman boxer and a male boxer is that a woman goes to her maternal side to bring out the killer instinct," explains Yolanda. "When a lioness protects her cubs, the fight becomes personal. The fight for a woman is personal; it has to be or she'll lose the killer edge. But two men, who were opponents in the ring, can go fishing, swap beers, or even become friends after the fight. Women seem to hold grudges."

I asked Yolanda, "What do you do with a dirty fighter?" Smiling, she replied, "I just hit them harder."

In September 2005, Yolanda was ranked in the top ten of the IFBA, WIBA, and the WBAN charts, right under Laila Ali, Anne Wolf, and Valerie Mahfood.

Malcriada Delilah Montoya Photographer

C. Ondine Chavoya

Delilah Montoya has engaged the power and beauty of photography for over twenty-five years. Montoya's visual art explores cultural history, memory, and identity through an approach that is both documentary and narrative. She works in a variety of two-dimensional photographic and printing processes as well as creating multimedia installations. Equally experimental and reverential, Montoya's images are densely textured and provocatively layered with aesthetic, spiritual, and political meanings.

Throughout her career, the artist has used documentary strategies to represent and interpret both contemporary and historical issues, typically in a synchronic process. This method has required that Montoya redirect the traditional documentary method and critically assess the cultural role and efficacy of photography. Through her art, Montoya critically re-imagines Chicana/o cultural and spiritual traditions to harness their liberatory potential and as means to combat historical erasure and subjugation. As such, Montoya engages the past to activate the present—and implicitly the future—through photographic representations. Over time, the format and presentation of Montoya's art has transformed significantly, but what has been steadfastly consistent is the artist's rigorous commitment to exploring personal and social issues through larger historical and aesthetic frameworks. In this way, the social and conceptual nature of her work extends rather than distracts from the formal elegance and beauty of her photographs.

One of the most prolific and respected Chicana artists working today, Delilah Montoya was born in Fort Worth, Texas, and raised in Nebraska with deep roots in northern New Mexico through her mother's family. For the artist, Aztlán is her conceptual homeland, which she carries with her and from where she operates regardless of physical geographic location. Aztlán is a Nahuatl term for the ancestral homeland of the Aztecs in the north, thought to be the present-day southwestern United States. (According to myth, the Aztecs journeyed southward in the twelfth century to found the promised land, Tenochtitlán.) In the early stages of the Chicano civil rights movement, Aztlán was reclaimed as a symbol of nationalism, decolonization, and resistance. As Montoya's photographs reveal, Aztlán represents the spiritual unity among a people who see in their past a source of cultural affirmation in the present. This concept of Aztlán is historically and contemporaneously intertwined with *mestizaje*, the transcultural processes that bridge Spanish and indigenous precolonial cultural practices that are richly brought to light in Montoya's photography. The art of Delilah Montoya contributes significantly to the ongoing and necessary reconceptualizaiton of Aztlán with particular attention to the specificities of gender, sexuality, body politics, and knowledge.

Now assistant professor of Photography/Digital Media at the University of Houston, Montoya began her studies of art in the late-1970s at the Metropolitan Technical College in Omaha, Nebraska. During these formative years, she worked as a staff photographer for a newspaper in Waterloo, Nebraska. She moved to Albuquerque to continue her studies at the University of New Mexico, where she received a BA in Studio Art in 1984. While in school, she took a position as a medical photographer for the University of New Mexico School of Medicine, which she held for ten years. (The famed and controversial photographer Joel Peter Witkin also once worked in this office for a short period of time.) This arrangement enabled Montoya to support her studies and practice while combining her photographic skills with computer applications. The University of New Mexico provided ample creative and technical support for the artist, and Montoya pursued her graduate studies there while developing a national reputation. Montoya earned an MA with honors in Printmaking in 1990 and an MFA with distinction in Studio Art in 1994. She was one of five graduate students in the nation to receive a College Arts Association Professional Development Fellowship in 1993, the inaugural year of the award, to support her MFA thesis project, *Sagrado Corazón/Sacred Heart*.

El Sagrado Corazón/Sacred Heart series from 1994 is a collection of collotypes that explore the meanings of the Sacred Heart as a cultural icon through portraits of the Chicano community in Albuquerque. Montoya's historical investigation of this religious symbol connects the baroque world of European Catholicism with the practices of Aztec worship. According to the artist, "It is not purely Indian in content and never completely European in its form. Rather, it is a hybrid of two diverse cultures that clashed and bonded at a particular historic moment and created the foundation for religious syncretism." Photographed with an eight-by-ten view camera and printed using an early photomechanical process from the nineteenth century that virtually disappeared after World War II, the portraits are extremely rich in detail and subtlety of tone. Elaborately staged and stylized, these performative portraits ultimately express the personal desires and concerns ("the hearts") of the individuals photographed.

A signature project that would launch her into the national fine arts arena, *Sagrado Corazón/Sacred Heart* was exhibited extensively. Traveling from Albuquerque to the University of Alabama, Mars Artspace in Phoenix, Intersection for the Arts in San Francisco, and the Daniel Saxon Gallery in West Hollywood, *Sagrado Corazón/Sacred Heart* was showcased in solo exhibitions at each venue. Such exposure is incredibly rare for a recent graduate; thus this impressive reception attests to the remarkable power and resonance of Montoya's artwork.

Since then, Montoya has exhibited internationally in countries such as France, Japan, Mexico, Russia, and Ukraine. Montoya's work was featured in the groundbreaking traveling exhibition *Chicano Art: Resistance and Affirmation, 1965–1985* and the International Center for Photography's monumental enterprise *Only Skin Deep: Changing Visions of the America Self*. Importantly, her artwork is represented in the permanent collections of several prominent cultural institutions, including the Smithsonian American Art Museum, Los Angeles County Museum of Art, Houston Museum of Fine Arts, Bronx Museum of Art, San Francisco's Mexican Museum, and the Museum of Fine Arts, Santa Fe, New Mexico.

Her 1996 series *Shooting the Tourist*, highlighted in the exhibition *From the West: Chicano Narrative Photography*, documents the activities of tourists in the Southwest. The installation demonstrates how the tourism industry has contributed to—and continues to promote—the West as a domesticated myth. In an effort to return the gaze of the tourist, the documentary project depicts the tourist's search for the "West" as a routine sequence of quotidian and thoroughly predictable behaviors. In pursuit of the "authentic" and the "native," the tourists captured in Montoya's photographs merely reproduce the myths that have ultimately over-determined their quest from the onset.

A more recent project, *Sed: The Trail of Thirst* (2004), produced in collaboration with Orlando Lara, also engages the tropes of the Southwestern landscape. However, rather than focusing on human interaction with landmarks and locales, this project wields its expressive power by focusing on the absence of the human figure in the landscape. This powerful installation depicts the perilous migration route across the Arizona-Sonora desert and the omnipresent thirst for water experienced by migrants during their clandestine border crossing. The installation includes panoramic photographs documenting the desert landscape, digital photographic prints, found objects, and a video of the trail that crosses the Sonoran Desert from northern Mexico into Arizona and the Tohono o'odham Nation. Displayed on shelves in front of the photographs are a collection of objects left behind on the journey, including the mismatched shoes of adults and children and religious votive items—touchstones for spiritual sustenance and safeguards for a safe journey.

For artist Delilah Montoya, this cultural landscape represents "a contemporary middle passage." Between 1996 and 2004, more than 3,000 migrants perished along the border. A poster created for the installation features a list of some 200 found dead in the area that had recently been published in the *Arizona Republic*. The increasing borderlands fatalities has prompted local and national debate, in addition to interventions by various humanitarian groups and individuals who have diligently sought to reduce the death toll along the border by providing fresh water tanks and jugs throughout the crossing zone. These efforts are symbolized by five plastic water jugs that are displayed in the exhibition; their labels have been altered to represent the motivations for the hazardous journey and read (in Spanish): Opportunity, Family, Money, Work, Education. *Sed: The Trail of Thirst* honors the courage of the migrant experience and those who have sought to provide the migrants with aid by establishing the controversial mini-oases scattered throughout the region.

Saints and Sinners (1992) is a photo installation exploring the iconography of the *Hermandad* (a New Mexican penitential brotherhood derived from colonial Spain) as a type of visual alchemy that transmutes sin into purity. This duality of saints and sinners—and the associated themes of life, death, and salvation—is also powerfully depicted in Montoya's *La Guadalupana* (1998). Originally produced for an installation at the Musée de Beaux-Arts Denys-Puech in Rodez, France, *La Guadalupana* is a 15 ½-foot photomural. Shot with a large-format camera, the monumental image features a man faced away from the viewer, standing in front of metal bars, and posed with his hands behind his back in handcuffs. Emblazoned on his back is an elaborate and brilliant tattoo of the La Virgen de Guadalupe. The image effectively channels the sacred and the profane and transforms the physical space of a prison cell into a sacred space and the body of the inmate into an *ofrenda* or altar. The memorializing function of the installation becomes all the more palpable when you learn that the person portrayed, Félix Martínez, was killed in his Albuquerque jail cell shortly after the photograph was taken. In this instance, the paired relationship of saint and sinner has the capacity to transform the viewer before the image into the penitent.

In 2000, Delilah Montoya organized the exhibition, *Nuevo Me-Xicano: Contemporary Chicano Art of New Mexico*, for the Magnifico!

2003 Albuquerque, New Mexico
Ring Girl, Melissa Borzachillo at Sandia Casino

art space in Albuquerque. In describing her curatorial vision for the show to the *Albuquerque Tribune*, Montoya explained, "Our lived reality had never been expressed artistically. We are drawing on a collective memory—a memory of absence. We're trying to discuss things that have never been discussed." This statement poignantly conveys the aesthetic strategies and ideals that have traversed Montoya's artistic career and is particularly significant in her work focused on *Las Malcriadas*. This undertaking involves an interrelated series of photographic projects and installations that function to reclaim and refigure the so-called "monstrous women" of Chicano and Mexican culture, including La Llorona (the weeping woman), Lillith (first wife of Adam in the Old Testament Apocrypha), Malintzín Tenepal (mistress of and translator for Hernán Cortés, popularly known as "La Malinche"), and Doña Sebastiana (a female death figure).

La Llorona in Lillith's Gardens (2004) comprises two mesmerizing photographic murals 20' x 8' and 10' x 8' that bring together two archetypal figures thought to have betrayed their husbands and murdered their children. According to folklore, both Lilith and La Llorona continue to haunt the terrestrial realm as evil spirits. "These women were presented as monsters," Montoya proclaims, "constructed to send a lesson to young girls on how to behave or how they should feel about these sort of 'monstrous women.'" The installation provocatively explores the traditional double standards that determine appropriate behavior for men and women and invests these female archetypes with new meaning.

Doña Sebastiana is an allegorical icon of death, often simply called La Muerte. Associated with the Northern New Mexican Penitente Brotherhood, Doña Sebastiana is traditionally represented as a grimacing skeleton in a death cart wielding a bow and arrow. In the video installation *San Sebastiana, Angel de la Muerte* (2002), Delilah Montoya revamps the folk icon into a diva by granting her a "new persona so to reclaim her as a woman empowered." The video depicts the voice of God trying to convince Doña Sebastiana that she is perfect as the figure of Death as she barters for sainthood. The interactive components of the digital video allow the viewer to move between seeing the beautiful diva that Sebastiana sees in herself and the skeletal face she wears as Death. In both instances, Sebastiana is magnificently skillful in her negotiations and exceptionally seductive when she asks, "Would you like to dance a bolero with me?"

The Spanish word *malcriada* can be roughly translated as "poorly raised or brought up," and is associated with a litany of other vernacular terms such as *sin vergüenza* (without shame), *callejera* ("woman of the street"), and *hocicona* ("big [animal] mouth," that is, a woman who speaks up, talks back, or challenges authority). All of these scolding terms function as interdictions to reprimand unacceptable behavior and demarcate the boundaries of acceptable femininity. Enforced by the traditional forces of Catholicism and patriarchy, such idiomatic expressions privilege particular forms of femininity and comportment and impose a public/private split on the female body, one that sanctions the domestic (family and home) as the proper space for "respectable" femininity. The scornful designation of *malcriada* necessarily implies a contravention of "proper" gender roles and thus represents a transgression of the ruling social order and its implicit boundaries. For the artist Delilah Montoya, a *malcriada* fundamentally represents a woman who defies convention and refuses to conform to social norms; thus, she has reclaimed the maligned word, inverting its assumed negative connotations in the process. Delilah Montoya appropriates and reactivates the term *malcriada* as a resource that propels us to explore territories generally deemed taboo in Chicano culture and inspires us to eradicate imposed boundaries as they are crossed. In this respect, the fierce athletes featured in *Woman Boxers: The New Warriors* are exemplary *malcriadas*. Delilah Montoya honors the passion, courage, and strength of these trailblazing athletes who will continue to inspire us all for generations to come.

C. Ondine Chavoya is an assistant professor of Contemporary Art and Latina/o Studies at Williams College.

Delilah Montoya Curriculum Vitae

Born: December 10, 1955
Resides: Albuquerque, New Mexico, and Houston, Texas

Education
1994 MFA, (Distinction) Studio Art, University of New Mexico
1990 MA, (Honors) Printmaking, University of New Mexico
1984 BA, Studio Art, University of New Mexico
1978 Associate Degree, Commercial Photography and Art; Metropolitan Technical College, Omaha, NE

Teaching
2001–2007 Photography/Digital Media Assistant Professor, University of Houston
2000–2001 Photo I/II, Instructor; Santa Fe Community College
1998–2000 Studio/Photo, Harnish Visiting Professor, Art Department, Smith College
1997–1999 Studio/Photo, Visiting Professor, Film and Photo Department, School of Humanities and Art, Hampshire College
1994–1996 Art History/Studio, Gallery Director, Department of Fine Art, College of Arts and Letters, California State University, Los Angeles

Selected Exhbitions
2004 Common Ground: Discovering Community in 150 Years of Art, Corcoran Museum of Art, Washington, D.C.
2003 Only Skin Deep: Changing Visions of the American Self: Coco Fusco, International Center for Photography, New York
2003 The Burden of Specificity, Heard Museum, Phoenix
2003 Altered States: Digital Art, Gallery at University of Texas-Arlington
2002 Ahora: New Mexican Hispanic Art, Art Museum of the National Hispanic Cultural Center, Albuquerque
2002 Guadalupe En Piel: Works by Montoya, Instituto Cultural Mexicano, Los Angeles
2001 La Luz: Contemporary Latino Art in the U.S., Art Museum of NHCC, Albuquerque
2000 Revealing and Concealing: Portraits & Identity, Skirball Cultural Center, Los Angeles
1999 Works by Delilah Montoya, John J College of Criminal Justice, New York
1999 Recent Acquisitions, Museum of New Mexico, Museum of Fine Arts, Santa Fe
1998 Ida Y Vuelta: Twelve New Mexico Artists, Musee Denys Puech, Rodez, France
1997 Talk Back! The Community Response to the Permanent Collection, Bronx Museum of the Arts, Bronx
1997 American Voices, Latino Photographers in the U.S., Smithsonian International Gallery, Washington, D. C.
1997 El Sagrado Corazón/The Sacred Heart, MARS Artspace, Phoenix
1996 History as Influence: American Work from New Mexico, Soros Center for Contemporary Art, Kiev, Ukraine
1996 Chambers of Enchantment, CEPA Gallery, Buffalo
1996 El Sagrado Corazón/The Sacred Heart, Daniel Saxon Gallery, West Hollywood
1996 Refiguring Nature: Women in the Landscape, SF Camerawork, San Francisco

1996 From the West, Mexican Museum, San Francisco
1996 Intersecting Identities, USC Fisher Gallery, Los Angeles
1995 El Sagrado Corazón/The Sacred Heart, Intersection for the Arts, San Francisco
1994 Guadalajara International Book Fair, Guadalajara, Mexico
1994 El Sagrado Corazón/The Sacred Heart, Cafe Gallery, Albuquerque
1994 American Voices, Latino/Hispanic/Chicano Photography in the U.S., Fotofest, Houston
1993 Fiesta Artística de Colores Art Exhibition, Albuquerque Convention Center, Albuquerque
1993 The Friends of Photography Auction 1993, Ansel Adams Center, San Francisco
1992 Los Guardianes: Land, Spirit, and Culture: The Alcove Show, Museum of Fine Arts, Museum of New Mexico, Santa Fe

Traveling Exhibitions

2000–2003 *Arte Latino: Treasures from the Smithsonian American Art Museum*
El Paso Museum of Art, Orlando Museum of Art, Palm Springs Desert Museum, Museum of Fine Arts-Santa Fe, Oakland Museum of Art.

1999–2001 *El Papel del Papel/ The Role of Paper*
La Sala Central del Antiguo Arsenal de la Marina Española en la Puntilla, San Juan Puerto Rico; Taller Puertorriqueño and Brandywine Workshop, Philadelphia; Caribbean Cultural Center and Hostos University, New York; Mexican Museum and Yerba Buena Center for the Arts, San Francisco; Centro Cultural de la Raza, San Diego; New Mexico Hispanic Cultural Center, Albuquerque; Guadalupe Cultural Arts Center, San Antonio.

1990–1993 *Chicano Art: Resistance and Affirmation, 1965–1985*
Wight Art Gallery, UCLA; Denver Art Museum; Albuquerque Museum; San Francisco Museum of Modern Art; Fresno Art Museum; Tucson Museum of Art; National Museum of American Art, Washington, D.C.; The Bronx Museum; San Antonio Museum of Art; El Paso Museum of Art.

Selected Collections

Los Angeles County Museum of Art; Houston Museum of Fine Art; Mexican Museum, San Francisco; The Bronx Museum; Smithsonian Institute; Wight Gallery, UCLA; Stanford University Libraries; Armand Hammer Museum, Los Angeles; Museum of Fine Arts, Santa Fe.

Selected Publications

2003 "Secrets of Survival," *Pictorial Shifts*. Sandra Matthews. Staffordshire, England: IRIS.
2003 *Women Artist of the American West*. Ed. Susan R. Ressler. NY: McFarland & Co.
2002 "On Photographic Digital Imaging," Delilah Montoya. *Aztlán: A Journal of Chicano Studies*. 27/1 (Spring 2002).
2002 *Contemporary Chicana and Chicano Art: Artists, Work, Culture, and Education*. Tempe: Bilingual Review Press.
2001 *Arte y Minorías en los Estados Unidos: El Ejemplo Chicano*. Ed. José Luis de la Nuez Santana. España: Universidad Carlos III de Madrid.
2001 "Using a Cultural Icon to Explore a People's Heart," Delilah Montoya. *Nieman Reports* 55/2 (Summer 2001).

Grants
2005 Cultural Arts Council of Houston and Harris County
2001 New Mexico Art Artist-in-Resident, Gallup, New Mexico
1993 College Arts Association Professional Development Fellowship, New York
1993 Sacred Heart Research Grant, Southwest Hispanic Research Institute, Albuquerque

Selected Catalogs
2004 FotoFest H2004 *Celebrating Water; Tenth International Biennial of Photography and Photo-Related Art*. Houston, Texas.
2003 *Only Skin Deep: Changing Visions of the American Self*. Eds. Coco Fusco and Brian Wallis. NY: Harry N. Abrams.
2001 *Arte Latino: Treasures from the Smithsonian American Art Museum*. Ed. Jonathan Yorba. NY: Watson-Guptill Publications.
2000 *Revealing & Concealing: Portraits & Identity*. Los Angeles: Skirball Cultural Center.
1999 *Imágenes E Historia/Images and Histories: Chicana Altar-Inspired Art*. Ed. Constance Cortez. Medford, Massachusetts: Tufts University Gallery.
1999 *Nueva Luz*. Bronx: En Foco (a community visual arts agency).
1998 *Ida Y Vuelta*. Ed. Laurence Imbernon. Rodez, France: Musee des Beauz-Arts Denys-Puech.
1996 *From the West*. Ed. Chon Noriega. San Francisco: Mexican Museum.
1994 *FotoFest '94: The Fifth International Festival of Catalogues Photography*. Ed. Liz Branch. Houston, Texas.
1993 *Chicanolandia*. Ed. Robert Buitron. Phoenix: MARS Art Space.
1992 *Los Guardianes: Land, Spirit, and Culture*. Ed. Judith, Baca. Santa Fe: Museum of Fine Art, Museum of New Mexico.
1992 *The Chicano Codices: Encountering Art of the Americas*; Ed. Patricia Draher. San Francisco: La Tienda.
1990 *Chicano Art: Resistance and Affirmation*. Eds. Richard Griswold del Castillo, Teresa McKenna, Yvonne Yarbro Bejarano. Los Angeles: UCLA Wight Art Gallery.

Galleries
Andrew Smith Gallery, Fine American Photography (505) 984-1234; Santa Fe, NM. www.andrewsmithgallery.com
Photographs Do Not Bend (214) 969-1852; Denton, TX. www.photographsdonotbend.com
Patricia Correia Gallery (310) 264-1760; Santa Monica, CA. www.correiagallery.com

Web Links
Delilah Montoya Home Site: www.delilahmontoya.com
Women Artists of the American West www. cla.purdue.edu/WAAW/Ressler/artists/montoyastat.html
Its All About the Apple, Or is it? www.sla.purdue.edu/waaw/Ressler/Ressleressay1.html
Celebrating Excellence www.unm.edu/~finearts/about/publications/excell.htm#montoya
Trail of Thirst www.orlandolara.com/thirst